A REAL WITNESS TO PLANET NIBIRU CROSSING AND REAL PARALLEL TIME SLIP

ANCIENT SITES DISCOVERED

UFO ENCOUNTERS THREE BIGFOOT ENCOUNTERS

TRIBUTE TO MY TRUCKER FAMILY

TRUSTING YESHUA

DARRELL LOPES

PAGE PUBLISHING
Conneaut Lake, PA

First originally published by Page Publishing 2023

ISBN 979-8-88960-139-5 (pbk)
ISBN 979-8-88960-140-1 (digital)

Printed in the United States of America

Norwey spiral chapters

CONTENTS

DESCRIPTION

This book is an absolute true account of all my encounters. I am a sixty-six-year-old born-again Christian. I met my still-today wife in church thirty-five years ago. I do not make up stories or make up lies. I come forward now to share with the world. These are true accounts of UFOs up close, of Planet X, or Nibiru, crossing up close, an actual account of a time slip to our parallel universe. I share about uncovering a 2,100-year-old mound builder's site on President Obama's Peace Award Day, the same day as the Norway spiral. It is also about a very ancient site perfectly put in place with boulders to mark the year's solstice and also my three Bigfoot encounters and a short tribute to my brothers and sisters in the trucking industry. So I thought I should share these encounters for those who are not saved or just those who doesn't believe in God and his Word. They believe that aliens created us. Also, I add a little about my love for the Native Americans as being their spirit brothers. So if you want your socks blown off, get the book. I can pass any lie detector. I'm not a professional writer. I just felt you needed to know these things. Thank you. God is good.

Darrell

CHAPTER 1

LET'S GET TO KNOW MY FAMILY

I would like to start this book out with a little bit about myself. I'm a full-blooded Portuguese; both sides of my family tree are from the Azores. The lost city of Atlantis was my ancestors' home. Our people lived on what was left of it. But I came from three generations of owners, operators, and truck drivers. Grampa drove a 1928 Fageol truck and trailer. When the Depression hit, he gave up and went back to farming in Castro Valley, California. I remember him harnessing up the Clydesdale workhorses and using a 16" John Deere plow to get the farm ready for planting, and by the way, I did get a couple of rides in that old Fageol. It would still fire up and be able to be moved out of the way at times. I was very young at this time. I was born September 11, 1956. If you would like more info on my mom's side of the family, my cousin Dorris Marciel was the San Lorenzo historian for years. She wrote a book on the history on the history of San Lorenzo and Castro Valley, California, area. She also was born on 9/11. She loves history and the past. We share that connection. She's in a rest home now. I felt I should add her in this book; she also put me in her book.

About one of my dig sites, I was working my great-grandfather's old place up at Marciel Gate in the upper Castro Valley hills. He was shoot in the head by kids bird hunting in the 1920s. Ironic it would end up being a shooting range owned by the park district.

Marsha Monterago and Duane Lopes are my sister and brother. They have been an amazing source of support, and I'm proud to call them family. They've been amazing hard workers all their lives and have been a major inspiration in my life. I've been blessed with four sons, Josh Canada, Jason Canada, Darrell Lopes Jr., and Jacob Lopes. These boys know how to keep their hands on the plow and get the job done. My wife, Beth, I met thirty-five years ago in church. We're born-again Christians, and without her, my life wouldn't be whole. It has been a walk that I wouldn't change for anything, which brings up the point. I would like to make a book about God, star brothers craft, Planet X, sacred sites, and a walk in my life-trusting spirit.

Before I forget, I want to talk about Mom and Belinda, my sister. Belinda passed away in 1977. I was three years out of high school. She died from leukemia at the age of twenty-three. As some of you may know, treatments were just experimental for cancer. At that time, it was all free and very painful (guinea pig), and she just couldn't take it anymore. When she had her relapse, she was living with two married schoolteachers. One of them was her French teacher at Tennyson High School. All of us kids went to Tennyson High; they loved her. She was the kindest, sweetest thing on earth. She was a heavyset gal when we were little, and boy, she could throw a punch. Anyway, about halfway through her short life, she completely transformed into this angelic personality, and everyone wanted her around them. I was a little jealous of her at a very young age. Friends of the family gave her a beautiful palomino horse called Doly. She loved to ride in the parade.

So, Mom, I will say these few words. She would say, "It's time to take the bull by the horns." She was an absolutely amazing woman. A mother's love is hard to fully wrap my brain around. She deserves an entire book wrote about this woman's life. Dad was a big rig driver. He started driving a truck at the age of thirteen. By the time he was fifteen, he owned his own rig. He borrowed my grandma's house, wrecked the truck, and Grandma almost lost her house. Boy, things were different in those days. He was one hardworking man. I miss him. He knew how to make me learn.

A REAL WITNESS TO PLANET NIBIRU CROSSING AND REAL
PARALLEL TIME SLIP

I remember standing in front of my house facing west. It was a beautiful, warm early summer afternoon. It was so warm and a peaceful day. I began to have God's spirit clearly speak to me. I knew it was God but didn't recognize his voice. Yet I began to smile and wanted to hear more and more of this and didn't want him to leave. I wanted to hold on and not let go of this, knowing full well it would leave soon. He said these words: "You are not going to be like a genius. You are not going to be like these millionaires, but you have a good heart, and this is what I look for in a man. And you I love and will be with you always." And this was spoken only like a true God could say it. My feelings were not hurt. I felt like I could come back and visit anytime.

I've been a Christian for forty-one years, and I will die a Christian. But I'm going to blow your socks off in this short book. Let's start by saying I swear on my sister's and mother's sacred graves that every last word I'm writing in this book is the absolute truth. And I assure you I could pass any lie detector. So let's begin. I have tried to call many hosts of online talk shows, and most of them claim to be psychic, yet I try to explain what I have experienced and they act like I need a degree in college and it couldn't be possible that I could know what I'm talking about. Anyway, no matter—you're getting facts and eyewitness accounts from me.

Let's move on; we've got a lot to cover. I'll walk you up to the time of my actual sighting of Nibiru, or so-called Planet X. There are a few things I need to talk about to help walk myself into explaining what took place that day. I was led to study Chaco Canyon and do more research on these sacred old sites. They can tell us so much about the people of the past. I learned that Pueblo Bonito is the center place below, and above is Orion's Belt, its mirror image in the celestial skies. And these buildings lined up lead you to sacred sites all over the northwest. These sites are sacred because a spiritual rebooting takes place there. It's lined up with the celestial and earthly underground ley lines, creating a supercharged site day by day, rebooting your spirit, a virtual hotspot. I said I was a Christian and I am, but I'm also a spirit brother to the Hopi tribe. I'll try to get to that story in this book, but this is kind of work for me. Every three words, I have to look up the correct spelling. I'm just a humble retired freelance archaeologist, truck driver, prospector, and treasure hunter. I'm a semiretired treasure hunter. I'm very careful about what I dig up these days. I'm not sure the world is ready to handle these things properly. When the gold comes out, everything goes to hell fast.

CHAPTER 2

Building up to Planet X Crossing and Time Slip

Okay, so we finished our work in Chaco Canyon. I felt I needed to make myself a handheld sextant out of wood. I was given a plastic one by an old friend, but this one came out nice. I used a welder's helmet lens, Brownstein shellac. It came out beautiful. I think it's still in the shop somewhere. So I felt like getting up on the roof, shoot the sun during the equinox, and with just simple model paint jot it down on the chimney bricks and then do the same thing on next year's equinox. So this was between 2004 to 2006; I believe I've gotten it written down somewhere. I was off four degrees, and I thought, *What the heck is going on here?* So I called my friend. Her husband had been on Art Bell's *Coast to Coast AM* many times. I can't use names, but he worked at the Miami circle site, and the Hopi elders loved him. I'm calling people to get permission to use their names, but no one is calling back; everyone one is busy today. So I'm just moving around them and staying safe. I feel I've got to get this out for the young people. And once it's done, it's done, and I can move on. If you want to see what I look like, I have two videos on YouTube when I was selling my ORMUS at CalaverasAlchemy.com. So we are building up to an awesome once-in-my-lifetime event, and it is true—no lies. This is the real deal. I so wish you could have seen it.

Somehow, I was being guided by some unseen force but at all times not really thinking about what would happen a few years later. I just kept trusting God and living out my everyday life. Let me say God and being saved will always be my number one, my biggest and greatest supernatural experience. I call him Yeshua Sananda in respect for the Tibetan term, Jesus, the one who descended. I love all races. I love all spiritual people. I will not judge. Thou shall not judge, get it? And I will always share my mind-blowing supernatural salvation event, the best thing that ever happened to me. Lead them to Grandfather Spirit and to love and respect Mother Earth. Like a fine old Christian woman told me, a lot of people know Yeshua, but they do not know God. You must use your heart to discern what the spirit is trying to guide you with. I'm going to help you understand Jesus and being saved and also understand star crafts, parallel universes, and sacred sites. Do not throw the baby out with the bathwater. Have enough faith in Yeshua and his life-raising spirit power; he is God. Also, he will protect you and keep you safe from anything above or below. This way, you will not be just a Christian with his or her head stuck in the sand. We must see all people as equal; there is no one better than another.

And by the way, everything is not the devil. Again, use your heart and have some faith. Anyway, we got offtrack a little, so back to Nibiru. These degrees were offtrack a little at the next summer equinox, four degrees or so. Something was out of whack with our sun. I'll tell you right now, NASA and the Catholic Church knew what was coming. That's why the church built that observatory near Phoenix, Arizona. They wanted a heads-up at that puppy when it was up and over our sun, she and her dark dwarf satellites. Her huge, black bellowing atmosphere got my attention fast. I could see her black atmosphere as clear as looking at our clouds; it was that close. Now I understand how that rogue Planet Marduk was broken in half, torn apart. This rogue could have knocked us into oblivion; it took Planet Marduk and ripped half of her into the asteroid belt. The Planet X crossing was in the second week of October 2011; that was about two and a half months from the Mayas 2012 event. They weren't too far off, were they? I call it the rollover, not crossing, because as an eyewitness, that's what it looked like to me up and over the sun and gone. I surely wasn't the only one who saw it. There was a brother trucker who came up alongside me and looked startled. I'm sure he was wondering what my reaction would be to the big show. I just nodded. I was so proud and felt so at peace with the earth and God, so spiritually in love with life itself. God, I love this place. If I would have waved him over to stop and talk, exchanged numbers, etc., we would have been partners in this book now. I only had a small handheld CB, and it had dead batteries; the power cord was buried somewhere in the Peterbilt. I didn't care. I think both of us were in a little shock. It got much worse for me in the weeks to come. Even though I was prepared for this, it still made me very emotional trying to handle this. So that's why I'm writing the book because I absolutely know someone else saw all this. And you'll understand when I open up here and break it down for you. I'm sorry everyone couldn't see this; if they would have seen this, it would have been a real eye-opener.

Okay, let me give you a little update on what happened to me after I was at home from the trip. I'd made one trip a week to Arizona for about six and a half years working for Trimac Transportation out of branch 46 Hayward, California. I was with them with my own rig, pulling their tanker. I was there for about twenty-two years. Now you know I'm not just some lying sack of horse manure trying to tell a tall yarn. I drove a white 1994 378 Peterbilt with a 36" sleeper bought brand-new and custom-built for me, all manual. Thank you, Yeshua.

So I had to come to grips with telling my family what happened and what I saw or if I was just going to say nothing, stick my head in the sand, pretend like nothing ever happened, and cower down like some sick puppy. Well, it didn't take but a few seconds to realize I couldn't let my loved ones be harmed, unprepared for what might happen in the near future. And believe me, I know full well of the book *The Tenth Planet*. I've studied the book well. I felt led to download it on my MP3 player three weeks before this Planet X rollover. Remember, I shared with you earlier that I have been led since 2004. Also, NASA released a talk about a rouge planet, I think in 1993.

So anyway, I came home from that trip. I began running my dowsing charts, and I was picking up a few things, and also, I heard on the radio about Planet Elanen or some comet with a blue trail that was related to my Hopi brothers and sisters. It is awesome that a crossing happened on my birthday, 9/11.

Then about a week later, I found out that the Maya were predicting hell breaking loose and Nostradamus was predicting more trouble. All this I was picking up on my dowsing charts. First, the walls started to close in around me, and I was all alone with this. I think what I was going through I would not wish on anybody.

All these things were happening around this blue star Kachina. (Please study your Hopi prophecy.) And yes, I did make it to the place where the sun comes up, then I returned to my people, hint hint. So you see, with all these things happening, it definitely was getting my attention. So I began to prepare, but timelines can change, changing events all the time, so I still began to prepare, building a dugout, a strong fort out of railroad ties. My charts were saying there would be water levels rising to four hundred feet; it would be at my front door. We would be at 450 feet.

So can you start to understand what I was going through by myself? I'm just letting you in on what was personally happening to me, not all fun and excitement. Thank you, God, for all the things that happen in this life and all the courageous people coming forward, sharing their experiences. Stay strong, my brothers and sisters. I thank God the Pentagon finally came out of the closet about UFOs. I was getting old trying to understand people's thoughts. When I shared my UFO experience, heck, my last brother's star craft was no further than forty feet away. I will talk about it a little more in the book. I won't tease you like that. I'm giving you all I can in this one.

So I was storing canned food, any honey, things that would last over time through the nightmare. So after this doomsday even passed, it started to dawn on me that all these past events that didn't happen were just different timelines. This is when other time lines and events went a different direction. So now I was starting to feel relief in the air. But the bottom line, I did share with my family members and friends for years up and down the road with my big rig. It's been good and bad. I felt it was my duty to share because if in case someone tries to trick you or scare you that Planet X is coming to get you, it won't come around again for another 3,168 years. Its return is not 3,600 years; my charts show its return at around 3,168 years or so. I believe that the author of the book *The Tenth Planet* knew the real time frame of Nibiru's arrival. They couldn't have the people panicking.

And this brings up a good point. I would like to reflect on the Maya 2012 predictions. These scholars today know a whole lot and are extremely educated, but no one can really interpret a language that is thousands of years old without some kind of Rosetta stone. So I feel deep down that all of us have a real understanding of these things. If you put your heart into it and if you have the faith to gather learning and trust God, you'll go forward.

Reading the Bible as a Christian like I am is definitely all you need. God's Word and prophecy are wonderful. But what if you're like me who loves ancient history like the Samaritans' stories of Atlantis and lost civilizations from the ancient past and you just want to understand our real past history and you believe that the past will help us understand the future? Then be careful, my family of spirit—you just might get a whole lot thrown on your plate that you didn't expect. So like I've said, don't throw out the baby Jesus with the bathwater because he's all grown up now and he is an expert guide through this walk of life. Sweeping the truth under the rug is not smart. But it did make me a little uptight when they talked about Brother Enoch. God said he was his favorite, so why did they take him out of the Bible? Was it because of this little learning trip he took up in the celestials? Do not throw out the baby with the bathwater, so there, we have swept too many truths under the rug. And know we are being misled. It's best just to face the truth and deal with it. These writers of the Bible really messed things up for the young people. They think we were created by aliens. Horse manure, then who created the aliens? Let's move on.

CHAPTER 3

Time Slip to a Parallel Universe/ Planet X Rollover

Now because of the magnetic pull from Planet X, I experienced a time slip in my kitchen. So did another man. I can't give his name. I'm not going to take the chance of getting sued. I'm sorry. And you will know exactly who it was if you were listening to *Coast to Coast AM*. That night, he came on *Coast* saying he had some company over for dinner, and when they were about to leave, the clocks had changed and then changed back again, and it freaked everyone out. The same thing happened to me in my kitchen but much, much more. I'll talk you through it.

My wife, Beth, and I were at the bottom of the hill at the east end of the ranch. It's steep, so I took the Yamaha XT500 so I could get back up to the top for tools. EXT. She was using the weed eater. We had a little trouble, and I needed some tools to bring some drink down. This was around the time before or just after my encounter with the Planet Nibiru rollover. The energy was still heavy in the air, and it opened a parallel time jump. This is what happened. I was in the kitchen, and I just happened to look up at the clock and notice that the clock was fifteen or twenty minutes off. So I looked over at the oven clock, and it was fine, so now I was upset. I had to see which ones were right and take time to get time reset again, so I looked at both clocks several times. I reached up to grab the clock. And before

I could lift my head to grab the wall clock, it changed back, and I absolutely knew what happened. Somehow, my touch set it back to the present time line, grounded it if you will.

But that's not all that happened. I started to come out of the kitchen and make a left to go down the steps, and out of the corner of my eye, I noticed a woman coming up the stairs, and she made a left down the hall toward the bedrooms. She was dressed in all white, and I don't mind telling it made me stop dead in my tracks. I still had my peace about me. But I definitely saw her, no doubt in my mind at all. So I started walking down the hall and went in the bedrooms, looking in the closets; that started to give me a chill. So I stopped looking for her quick. So I said to myself, *Okay, Beth's waiting for me at the bottom of the hill. The weed eater's still broken. I've got to get back to her.*

I started to head down the stairs. When I reached downstairs, something told me to turn around and call out to her. Remember I told you I know I saw her, so I said out loud, "Are you there?"

And I swear on my sacred mother's grave, she said, "Yes, I am." Her voice was like it had a veil over it. I knew right away I was splitting to different parallel times. So that was enough for one day, and I jumped on the 1976 XT and back down the hill to Beth with supplies. And just because she was all dressed in white, I didn't pick up at all that she was a spirit. Believe me, I've been a Christian over forty years; I know a spirit when I feel it. She was about 5'5" tall with short black hair, and the clothes she was wearing were like a nurse's uniform. I went down and told my wife about it. She didn't say much, so I didn't say anything more about it.

Two weeks later or so, that's when that guest on *Coast to Coast* came on, talking about a time slip with his clocks. I don't keep military logs for date and times; I'm just going on my memory, sorry. I have tried to contact him and no reply. I guess God didn't let it get out. He waited till I could write the book. I guess I would have shared this with the right team anyway. I am not into the money game; I totally just want an honest fair share.

It's been eleven years since the Planet X crossing, and speaking of that nurse in white, I remember asking my neighbor if the woman who lived in my house before me worked in a hospital. He replied no. If I could do it all over again, I'd have a thousand questions to ask her. That was one chance in a lifetime. The veil closed. That was definitely one of my top fifty greatest encounters, and I feel kind of privileged to have seen and heard it. Having all these events happen has helped me to understand myself. I believe God let me experience all these events in my life. He knew that my faith in Yeshua, God the Father, and the sacred Holy Spirit would never let go astray. I don't think I've ever contemplated that there was no God. I have never seen him, but I sure as heck have felt him. Thank you, Holy Spirit. I have wondered many times since that day when I talked with that woman in a parallel universe if they absolutely know that there is at least one parallel universe running side by side with ours. I wonder how long I could have kept a conversation going with her. My God, at least her name would been cool. Einstein was right, and so was the author of the book *The Tenth Planet*. So you see how I'm trying to help you weave truth with truth.

And hold your ground, my brothers and sisters. Yeshua did walk this earth, and I'm convinced that he walked this earth more than once. The Cherokee speak of him coming to them and saving their tribe from a natural disaster. They called him the god of the wind and water. I'm almost ready to devote myself to you nonstop on what happened that day with the Nibiru rollover. I'm sorry. I'm not holding off. There's just so much to get off my chest, but please have patience. This is a very important event in history. Okay, let's take it from the beginning to the end of that amazing, wonderful, scary, beautiful, ten- to twenty-minute once-in-3,176-year event. I unloaded in Glendale, Arizona, and I was on my way back home. I headed west on I-10 around Tonopah, Arizona, the whole day.

It was like when I was a YACC (Young Adult Conservation Core) at twenty-three years old, stationed in Dorrington, California, forest service. I pulled a two-year stretch. It was cloudy, and the clouds were filled with lightning. We used to call it lightning strike season. We got paid double time. The guys all looked forward to this season. The first thing I noticed was what I could only describe as what looked like a tornado without the spiral turns in it; it went all the way up in the sky and was all the way to the ground. I might add it was partly transparent, almost like some kind of reflection from the sun.

Next were two suns ready for sundown, one sun in the back of the ether. The sun in the back of the other sun was peeking out about 15 percent; you could definitely see two suns. It was getting close to sunset. My explanation for this, from thinking about it for some time, is people around the world were seeing two suns. But their suns were farther apart than when I was there. This is because Nibiru was about to head up and over our sun and then go. See how important this book is. This was an amazing celestial event that ancient people recorded. And I was an up-close eyewitness. They could make a cool movie out of this event. I'm really hoping someone reads this and is near me out there and will come forward. Most folk don't know what they are looking out for. Even though I was prepared for this since 2004, it totally caught me off guard. It took years before I could write this book. The information had to be slowly digested over time. It was a lot for anyone to take in, trust me.

So next, I saw the red-hot winded globe. It was like one more sun. I thought to myself, *How could anyone survive on that thing?* Everything was happening so fast. No time to do anything, just watch. Then next was the swirling tornado of gold particles. This was absolutely beautiful, this golden mass of gold particles; you could see it was charged with electricity. It filled the whole sky, swirling like an out-of-control tornado then was up and over the sun and gone. I knew what I was looking at way deep down.

When I'm discovering treasure or ancient sites or dealing with star crafts, Bigfoot, or anything dramatic, a peace and calmness falls on me, which I am grateful for. Then there were Nibiru's satellites; I only saw one, but I'm sure there were more. It came up like in short segments of a kind of moving picture. At first, it was like holding a basketball at arm's length right in front of you. Then in about three or four segments, it reached its max height; it absolutely filled the entire sky. This burned-out dwarf star or whatever was massive, and I could see its black cloud atmosphere right up in my face.

We're having a huge lightning storm while I'm writing this chapter, and it's perfect for this chapter. It's November 9, 2022, and a full moon too. I'm also watching a PBS documentary, *Chaco Canyon*. It's perfect to write, a writer's dream. I will say this now. I believe when the next Planet Nibiru comes around, my gut feeling tells me with that crossing, there might be trouble. Somehow, this will be the last time we get a big second chance; let's make the best of it.

So when the dark satellite was filling the sky, I could clearly see its atmosphere; this thing was really close. It looked just like our clouds, but these were billowing up like some kind of a volcano. I was definitely not our friend, a horrible black billowing nightmare and way too close.

CHAPTER 4

The Reason No One Saw Planet X Crossing

Now I will talk about why everyone all over the world didn't see Planet Nibiru crossing. I'll explain this way. If they launched the space shuttle from Cape Canaveral in Florida and you were in San Francisco, the shuttle could climb up and out of our atmosphere. You couldn't see it; maybe at night, it would look like a satellite but not in the daytime. It is the same if you could stretch the Eiffel Tower up one thousand times higher. Night or day, you couldn't see it from far away. And Planet X crossed over our sun at sunset, making it impossible to see. You had to be in that right place at the right time and also at the right trajectory of its crossing. This is why the Catholic Church spent all that money to build that observatory near the University in Arizona. Think a bit about what I just said. I believe one of the untold secrets of Fatima gave them a heads-up; this is why the cash rolled out for the observatory.

Half my family comes from the Azores Island, and the other side comes from St. George. I'm full-blooded Portuguese, so in one way, I'm very grateful. For having a bird's eye view of it, on the other hand, it has been very disappointing to not have someone else to share this with. At times, it's almost lonely, so I'm writing this book. I'm sixty-six years old with diabetes for thirty years. Heck, I do not know how long I'll be on this plane of existence. And there's been never a dull moment.

Life is a gift. We must be grounded and right with God and our Mother Earth. This world is designed like a Swiss watch. Our bodies resonate at 7.83 Hertz. So does Earth's gravity frequency. We need to be balanced with gifts of the Holy Spirit: kindness, love, peace, joy, and things of the spirit. If you are doing bad, treating people dishonestly, and only caring about yourself, you are out of balance with spirit and the earth. This type of person will not grow. We must be balanced like our beautiful world. You were created for this starship Earth, and it's never too late to change. Let's make this second change around our beautiful sun count this time. Let's get it right.

We call ourselves Northwest Treasure Solvers; there's five of us. I've been blessed with the gift of finding things lost for hundreds of years, even a thousand years back. I will try to share with you a couple of things. We were looking for a good archaeologist to help with getting permits. We pinned down Drake's hoard or what's left of it. It's on the coast; it's federal land. We stay in the light and balanced, no shady bull crap. But let me walk you in slowly to our 2,100-year-old mound builder site. We located this site on President Obama's Peace Award.

CHAPTER 5

Norway Spiral and 2,100-Year-Old Mound Builder's Site

Remember the Norway spiral was on that same day I located this site. Okay, stop. Let me back up a little with the Nibiru rollover. Planet X rolled over our sun, not our planet, making it that much harder to spot from Earth.

Okay, let's continue on the day of Obama's Peace Award. I was staying at my mother-in-law's house for six months. So when we bought this house, it was a total wreck. We got it cheap, so between trucking loads, I would go out hiking a short chance to get out of that truck. So I was hiking on that day and was up at Lake Chabot and was led to a 2,100-year-old sacred mound builder's site. If you slow your steps way down and begin to listen to the past and the earth blocking out everything else out, the earth and the past will begin to speak to you. We all have this gift. I was led to some buried rocks and was told to look closer to them and move the grass away. I noticed some very old carved symbols on these rocks.

By the way, I have some nice eight-by-ten shots. I'll try to get them in this chapter for you. So I sent those shots to the Smithsonian Institution; they loved the pictures and wanted to help me. We talked a couple of times on the phone; they were very nice. But they didn't have the funds to help me out.

So I was at my mother-in-law's house; she's an amazing lady, one of a kind. Running my dowsing charts, it helped me understand the site. Dowsing is a form of remote viewing, nothing more. It spoke of a Maya connection to this site, also a mound builder's site connection. This is a place where there are heavy underground ley lines intersecting, creating a supercharged, powerful place. I believe they could teleport to a different time space. It also turned hard rock into soft putty, making it simple to make their carvings in the rock. Look closely at my shots; you'll see they look unique in themselves. I believe they also used sound vibration in a way; maybe Coral Castle was a similar technique. Anyway, my charts indicated that I was to hike up to the top of the hill. There would be a vortex site and also a collapse chamber there. Also, there would be old ones who would be buried there.

It did turn out there were two parents and two children buried there. Trust me, no one will ever know where they're resting. These folks were the tall ones. My Hopi brothers and sisters want their grandfathers to rest, and rest they will. Amen. I am also caretaker of a giant's burial ground. It's in the eye of an ancient burned-out volcano, the one I call Grampa. He's fourteen feet, ten inches tall. No one will ever know this site either. We must learn how not to cash in on our past. At this site, these people were good folks. North of this site is a place called the Devil's Playground. These giants were not so nice, and that's putting it mildly.

Okay, so I went to the top of the hill and looked around and noticed a short tree twisted like a drill bit. I walked over there with both my two copper dowsing rods as I walked toward the corkscrew tree. When I got close, a few feet away, they crossed. I knew right away this is where two ley lines met up. I might add whenever I'm right in that spot with my eyes closed, hummingbirds start buzzing around my head. So now my charts were leading me to the back of this twisted tree around this vortex area around the heavy brush loaded with poison oak. Now I lined myself up with the corkscrew tree. I was about twenty-five feet from it; on the other side of it, over the brush, you couldn't see it. There at my feet was the collapsed chamber that had caved in a long, long time ago. I believe they would climb down in it and have their ceremonies with the power of their learned technology combined with the ley lines, accompanied by sound or instruments. They would move themselves to a different time space, one of the first jump rooms if you will.

I believe back at the half-buried rocks, there are a ton of rocks with symbols. I would love to set up and have a professional archaeologist set up a dig with our group right there, keeping an eye on the goodies. That would be cool to uncover another Rosetta Stone to help us find out what was going on there. We need more info. We do not have enough ancient Rosetta Stones if you will. The knowledge these people had must have been off the charts. So over time, I began to work on the hillside next to the half-buried stones with all the glyphs on them. I found many just half-buried under the dirt. So I came up with a plan to gather up all I could find and get with the park head ranger. And when I had enough proof, I'd get him out there to have a look.

And before anyone says I should have not touched anything, I'll tell you right now I've been a freelance free spirit archaeologist since 1983, and how many times do you think I've talked to universities and archaeologists asking, pleading for help only to be laughed at or hung up on? One character was so rude to me over the phone. I had visions of going over to his house at three in the morning and toilet-papering his house. I was hot. I'm sorry, but I've had enough of these so-called experts. Some are downright strange. They don't have enough common sense to hear a man out and be able to understand people like the Hapi tribe that just know things that you can't learn in any school.

Okay, so I gathered up all I could possibly find and hid them the best I could in plain sight, and then I brought out the park ranger in charge. Before this happened, I got my VHS out on the site and got everything down before they could grow legs. I've got over an hour on tape of all of it. I'm glad I did to get a time set with the park district to meet out at the site. The park ranger was super nice. He was a great guy. I made him a copy of the VHS and dropped it off at the station before we met. But he wasn't there. There were a couple of young workers there, but when we were out there together, he asked me what I would like done here. I told him we needed to get a professional archaeologist in here, fence off everything, get to work, and in the end, it would be cool for the kids if we would set up a learning place with benches and tables and teach the kids. And throw in a snack bar—that would be sweet. It would be a nice field trip for our young people. However, nothing happened. I think someone else got that VHS because one by one, those artifacts were taken. And before I forget, this site is located up at Lake Chabot, Regional Park Headquarters off Lake Chabot Road, Castro Valley, California.

As a young boy, I had been horseback riding many times there. We would race the horses there and then ride back to the ranch. Grampa's ranch was back on Seven Hills Road in Castro Valley. They had a roadside vegetable stand out front. This was where Grampa parked the old Fageol truck and trailer. It was a three-and-a-half-acre ranch that dated back to the late 1800s. Now there are seven homes on it. They call it Marciel Ct. It sold back in the early eighties, and by the way, when I got back from running those saddle horses up at the old site, my grandmother had a yell that was more like a shriek, something I never wanted to deal with.

I'm sorry for digressing from the site; it's the only way I can give you a little of me. It's all connected. I just know that there's so much that the past can help us with in the future; it heals us. And I want to say this also: The closest thing to Jesus I've ever seen or experienced is knowing the Hopi tribe. They are kind and gentle; they love the earth, water, air, and sky. We can learn a lot from them. They do not speak with a split tongue. Their hearts are grounded to Mother Earth. They put themselves last and mankind first. They understand life is a gift and responsibility is not a way to make a paycheck. Let's get our lives balanced again.

There are a lot of really cool people in this world. I've been blessed to meet them. I will say 95 percent of the folks I've met in the trucking world and everywhere else were great folks. I've always loved being around older people especially as a young boy. I felt blessed from their wisdom. I could relax around them. So I learned a lot when I was young like never bring back the horses all lathered up. Gram would have kicked our butts. So who would have ever thought that the same place where two kids would be hanging out smoking cigarettes and grazing their horses, fifty-three years later, I would uncover a lost sacred site 2,100 years old? I sure didn't. We were as close as twenty-five feet of those half-buried rocks. They called this part of Chabot the old Niki Base.

Anyway, I find it fascinating that I located this vortex site on the day of the Norway spiral and Obama's Peace Award; there is no coincidence in life. If we ever get a good archaeologist that we can trust, maybe I'll write about it and reopen the site. There's a lot to uncover there. Lots of ancient symbols are still underground to understand and digest.

So I think I will slowly move on to one of my UFO sightings in 2000. I might add we have a prehistoric site fairly close to our home; it's somewhere near Lake Camanche. This site was on EBMUD land. The site was located by one of their workers. There were lots of really cool complete dino skeletons. By the time we found out in the local paper, it was all gone and neatly put away. This is what I mean about being very careful how you deal with these sites. We are very careful now before we bring anyone aboard. Northwest Treasure Savers have a good committee; no fly nights are allowed. We learn from our mistakes. We will not be taken advantage of again. I would just as soon leave things buried for another thousand years. I'll wait till people understand how sacred and special these sites are for our young people to learn from. There is no room at all for coveting. So let's get into my 2000 UFO sighting that was one of my top five biggest, coolest awakenings in my life. See you in Chapter 6.

CHAPTER 6

2000 UFO Encounter

Let's begin this one with when I was making my first trip of the year of 2000. My Peterbilt, only six years old, had no sleeper. When I was younger, I just lay across the seats. I could take that then. That went on for about twenty years, then I said, "No more, no way." Okay, this was the first week, the first trip of January, my first trip of the New Year. I was headed for Dunn Edwards, Phoenix, Arizona. I had five thousand gals of latex for them; it was a great place to be.

Anyway, I started out from the bay area. I used to leave the yard around 8:00 p.m. I was headed south on Highway 99 right down by the truck scales in Chowchilla, California. Back in the day, on the old highway just past the scales, there's kind of an S-turn with a small dirt lot for a very quick pullover. It's gone now. The highway was rebuilt with just a straight shot through that area now. So I was headed south, and I noticed what looked like a comet about half a mile up and following the slow lane. It looked like about a mile up in the air, and the first thing that went through my mind was, *Man, that's cool. I haven't seen a good comet since 1997 Comet Hal-Bopp.* Well, that was short-lived. This comet began to make a U-turn to the right. Now I was thinking, *Oh boy, now we're on time for a cool learning process, and this one's about time.*

Then it started to come back to me about two hundred feet up in the air and four hundred feet to the right of the slow lane. Then about a quarter mile away coming at me, well, I also knew this was going to be a top 10 event in this one's life, that was for sure. I was one big raging ball of fire, so I made use of that short, quick dirt pullout. I jammed her over quick and hit the air brakes. Now over the years, I've realized this was all planned out by them. I didn't think about that till writing this true story. It was their time to meet, not mine. I've known always I was being watched out there late at night running out in that beautiful desert. God, I miss that.

Please forgive me—I have to digress a little bit again. I'm watching another Chaco Canyon documentary. They're convinced that the people at Chaco Canyon were cannibals. Let me say if you have any knowledge at all of the complex engineering over hundreds of miles that these people were cannibals. I've got a bridge for sale. Let's explain. They were invaded by hybrids, half-human, half something else, similar to the red-haired giants of Lovelock, Nevada. There's a war going on now and back then. Remember we talked about the Devil's Playground. Thank you, Yeshua, for being you. These hybrids were attracted to these energy sites. There was a lot of energy that attracted good and not so good. It will get heavy in two number one star crafts.

Let me digress some more—thank you. Let me say these hybrids were after a quick meal also. Like my people, the Christians, if you're worth your grain of salt, you can bet you've gotten knocked down more than once. There was a war going on at Chaco back then, and it's still going on. This part of the book is dedicated to my Native American family and also my family of brothers and sisters, the Christians. Spirit is truth and light. The energy that comes and goes in this man cave is off the charts. It is for this reason I digress. You're going to get both barrels in this book; the spirit is in control.

Okay, back to this ball of fire. I was parked in the dirt pullout. I had a pair of binoculars hung on my hat hook on the passenger side window. Just as the ball of fire got right in the wing window so I could see it, by the time it took to throw up my binoculars, this ball of fire, this comet, instantly turned into this football field-sized triangle star craft that was there. It was shaped like an Indian arrowhead. This triangle-shaped craft had a small tail to it like an arrowhead that had a part to tie it to the shaft. And this was not one of those funky man-made triangle-shaped UFOs. A breath away, it looked like it came right out of *Battlestar Galactica*. Absolutely beautiful. All my anger built up over the years dissolved in a heartbeat. I had a lot of anger built up about these unknown star brothers taking eggs from women. I was ready to get out of my truck and kick their butts or die fighting. I felt this was God's country and I was, and still am, one of his warriors, and if you think I'm not a Christian, you better think twice. I will fight to the death if God calls for it. Now you're getting a little portion of Darrell.

But several things were happening. One thing was they took my fear and anger away. As I looked and studied this for just a few seconds, it placed a hologram of the three pyramids of Giza. This caused me in a split second to have a great, overwhelming peace. And this boss of the celestials had taken time to let me know that yes, they were here and that I was not to be afraid, that they knew me and that we could mind-speak together. I instantly knew what this galactic star craft was going to do.

Meanwhile, remember it was the beginning of the second week of January of 2000, and I was standing outside in front of the Peterbilt at night freezing my butt off, and I couldn't take too much more of it, and I got to run down all the way to Mohave for my layover. So let me say more about this Battlestar Galactica of peace. For one thing, it was the size of a football field. It could stop completely and make no sound or wind or anything, and I think this ball of fire served two purposes. One was it could mask or cloak itself as a comet. And two, it somehow used that ball of fire to reenergize its power source using the sun and gravity field to power up. This is all I got out of that. It had windows. It was flat black in color. I can't remember the lighting colors—maybe a few colors, mostly clear white type of LED lights—but I could see it very clearly at night. She made absolutely sure of that. I told everyone. Let me say if I would have had my father's 30-06 with its scope on it, I could have blown the windows out of her. That's how close I was to her. I don't think that would have been a good idea, considering it looked like it'd been around for thousands of years and they were showing themselves to me as friends. So I spoke out loud to it and said, "I know what exactly what you're going to do next. I'm going to climb back up in my warm baby, and I'm going to jump back out in that slow lane. And as soon as I start out, you're going to swing around behind me and head out above both sides of the freeway. And then you're going to swing back around and right back into that small dirt pullout where you first uncloaked from the comet fireball." And off I went, and sure enough, that's exactly what happened.

This what I'm talking about. There was mind-speak going on here. But this didn't end there, so I headed down to Tipton, California, a rest area. I was bushed and couldn't make it over the Tehachapi Mountains, where my spirit Kachinas lived. On the next day, I started out pretty early and turned on the local news to find out if someone must have seen this event. No one traveling in the area could have missed it. Sure enough, it came on local news radio that several folks had called in reporting this so-called comet. That made me feel a little better, but it made me have to process a whole bunch of other things. So to put it mildly, I just moved on; I had a sweet load to deliver.

I need to stop right now and just say this sighting didn't shake my faith in God. I was geared for this event. Do not throw the baby out with the bathwater. I'm so grateful I knew Yeshua first and all these other cool things would happen after. I was rooted in deep to Mother Earth and Yeshua and the awesome power of the Holy Spirit. Now you see why I'm writing this for the whole world to understand that you do not lose faith in God. The problem is that the writers of the Bible left out or was taken out too much that they didn't understand or felt they would lose control of the people. So this is why a lot of people not grounded in God's Word will be missed.

So anyway, I went home and drew up some sketches on what happen. I told everyone what went down. They didn't say too much, so I just kept working got to keep those paychecks rollin' in about a year and a half. I was kicking back on the weekend by the fire. I love my fires. I'd burn through two cords a year. And on the TV camera news show about UFOs, and they were showing a live video on the east coast. They were right in that timeframe three or four days after I had my big show. There they were talking about triangle-shaped

UFOs that shook up a lot of home owners, truck drivers, and local police departments. They had news reporters and the whole works on live local television. I was taken back. It was good to know that someone else saw what I'd have gone through. I'm glad my encounter was much more peaceful. My second encounter was much closer but definitely was not as beautiful. I'm writing this book not to promote UFOs. There's probably going to be an increase in UFOs in the near future, so I don't want you to be shaken to the core. And I believe you were lied to about the past history and the Bible. You'll need the power of the Holy Spirit to determine if they're good or evil. You do not want to end up as a human smoothie drink, so I'll end this encounter by saying.

CHAPTER 7

SECOND UFO ENCOUNTER

I really wish everyone could have seen this absolute marvel of the Celestials, maybe you will someday. Okay, will start out with the beginning. I was on my MAGNATRAC RS 1000 miniature bulldozer, cutting a new hiking trail for Beth. I was heading west back up the hill trying to keep my butt from sliding off the seat it was steep. I couldn't let go of the steering controls that was the only thing that was holding me in. I remember having to keep going. I was trying to make it to the flatter part of the trail. Suddenly, I felt a burning sensation in the right side of my stomach. I could not let go, and it just kept burning. It hurt like heck for a second. I thought a black widow had got in my Carhartt overalls. We had some huge ones up here in the gold country, and then I realized I was being hit by some kind of a scaler weapon. I looked up and knew it was coming from the two o'clock position so the following day, I had a load from Bear Manufacturing, another load of latex. I made it about to Westley, and I had to pull over. I was getting really sick, and brother, I knew I was in for big trouble by the time I got empty in Santa Ana, and I thought I wasn't going to make it home again. I remember calling my big brother. I told him I loved him I was talking out of my head. I really thought I wasn't going to make it back to the ranch.

I was on fire, and at least I could say goodbye to at least him. I had him shaken up. He had always looked out for me when I was little. I pulled out of Santa Ana and made it up to Lebec, California.

I had to pull over. I had to lance my wound. It felt like it was going to explode, so I made it home to the safety of my bed. I was off work for about seven days. I had high fever for a week. My son, little Darrell, was up for his vacation. He spent his whole vacation at the ranch. He wouldn't leave my side. He knew I was in bad shape.

Now here goes the UFO experience. I was getting better. It was about 3:45 a.m. Let me say I did get to the doctor by that time. I had black and clear fluid running out of my wound. Sometime during the time of high fever about 3:45 a.m., my room lit up like someone was outside with their high beams on waking me up. I was furious. I got up and went to look outside the window peeking out the blinds not to give myself away. What I saw was no more than forty feet from my bedroom window hovering over our street about four feet off the ground. It was roughly the size of a Volkswagen bug, but it was turned sideways to me. There was no sound. Now it made sense to me about getting hit in the stomach with some kind of scalar weapon from the 2:00 p.m. sky.

It had four basketball-sized main running lights side by side, two by two except there was a ring of small LED lights around the four main lights like some kind of cool front car grill. The front four main lights look just like the craft that rose up behind the driver in the work truck at the railroad crossing. In *Close Encounters of the Third Kind*, it was exactly the same width and size. Except no colored small lights, it really puzzled me for a moment then there was a huge flash of light like the strength of the sun, almost blinding, but it flashed me so fast that it wasn't too bad. The power of that light flash was definitely enough power for it to bend space-time to a parallel universe. I want to stop and say the doctor had taken a test sample of my wound, sent it in, and it came back with a staph infection. So I'll never know if that star craft was there to check in on me or just stopping by to watch me suffer. I'll never know I'm still open to both thoughts. I don't hold any grudge.

So that's about the short and long of it. So you can understand this sighting was totally more involved than my 2000 encounter. I'm glad to be able to bring these encounters of my personal experiences with these star people. So now you can see, Christians have had to go through these kinds of events and not be struck down in their faith in God, Yeshua, and the Holy Spirit. I feel blessed with this life and wouldn't change any of it. I have come forth with real in-your-face events in my life that I feel must get out in the public to help the young and old to understand things that are very, very hard for some people to digest. Anyway, I loved the way both crafts looked. It was totally, unbelievably real. I will never forget and need no notes to write this book. My thoughts are, How and why would you worry about what life has to throw at you when the spirit of the creator of this dream and galactic, celestial star friends are looking out for you? Why would you worry? You already know that nothing is by coincidence. And I mean all different time lines are under Gods complete control. This world is his footstool. What we've got going on here at the ranch is a caretaking of the local deer. The ones that are injured, sick, or shot up, they know there's help here there's no fences. The deed made me take them all down. We are the deer people. We must give back to the land and hold ourselves accountable in this life for our actions as a human being. I was not thinking of just me and my family but everyone on the planet. I was praying for all people, wanting the best for all mankind.

I often wonder how great this planet would be if we all shared the resources fairly. How cool this earth would be and we could grow—that means all of this world. There would be no wars, just brothers and sisters all over the world working for the good and well-being of all. This is the way to go forward. This planet would be known as the apex of the celestials. We together would be known out of the galaxy as the true peacemakers of the universe.

My words to the young people would be "Get off the drugs. Drugs are for people in a hospital. You are spirit beings. Don't let the dark spirits take advantage of you." As Mom would say, "It's time to take the bull by the horns." Miss you, Mom. Take back your right to be a human being, and tell the dark half to go pound salt. Now make a slave out of it. You have an important role in life just being you. The whole world would grow in prosperity, not just haves and have-nots. Our spaceship called Earth would be back in balance, and this world would bring a higher frequency like your car tires when it's straight out of the balancing shop. Everything runs smoother, and if you're a brighter person and good in business, you make more money. It is not a sin to be bright, and if you are a bright person and also balanced, think of the good that you could do for the less fortunate, helping people, expecting nothing. Think what could be done on the Native reservations. These Native Americans are the salt of Mother Earth. They need a blessing paid back for all the small-pox blankets handed out, the land, their families stolen from them. When we bless them, then the earth will be blessed.

How can we help? Well, for starters, our family donates to the Northwest Indian Foundation. In New Mexico, for 560, you can purchase a wood and coal stove, so Grandma and Grampa up on the reservation do not have to use a fifty-gallon drum to heat their home. When Grandma and Grampa are warm, then we will be warm. We can correct the mistakes of the past. We can heal the people of the land, then the land will heal all of us. When I was a young boy of six or seven, Grampa would pick corn on the farm with a workhorse and a tall, narrow sled. I would jump on the back of the runners and get a free ride. But there was one morning I remember reaching up and pulling down the corn pollen and knowing something about this was very special, sacred but not knowing. Something in my mind said, *Darrell, someday you will understand.* Well, I did find out years later. Let's go in to discuss in a simple way about human beings, technology, computers, etc.

If you were born from a computer somehow, if there was a computer that made human beings, then your mother would be a computer and your ancestors would be technology. But you're not made of a computer chip; you're made of Mother Earth and your mother and father were made of the earth, so why would we serve technology and wealth and put these things first in your life? Why would you put money first and not listen to the heartbeat of your mother the earth and grandfather spirit Yeshua and his spirit? So did I help you in understanding the ways of the Native Americans, and why I call them brothers and sisters? Whom do you want to serve, computers, technology, or great wealth? Why not love our God and Yeshua and our beautiful earth? Let's get balanced. It's time to understand the stories of the Native Americans without judgmental thoughts. Lose the ego. If you listen carefully, you will hear with your spirit they are talking about the same God. We all serve the same God but not the dark half. Our God is God over peace, kindness, patience, love, joy, caring, and discipline. You must learn to listen to the stories with an open heart, with no judgment. Thou shall not judge, and the light of truth will explode with brotherhood like a new spring day.

When everything takes off and grows, it gives some kind of fruit that will come forth, so do not let commerce, wealth, and material stuff come first. Your Mother Earth is a trillion times more powerful and is your ship of life around our sun. So let's treat her with care and respect. Take care of your Mother Earth. Remember, she rotates at one thousand miles an hour and we travel sixty-seven thousand miles an hour around the sun. That wouldn't take very much for her to buck us off and turn us into stardust. We would be vaporized in less than a second if we lost our gravity field, and I've seen the rogue planet that could do it. Let's keep praying this planet into balance. God is good. What an exciting time to be alive, amen. We're going through a power outage right now. This is January 8, 2023. Remember the California bomb cyclone. Well, it hit us right now. All I need is another candle and a feather inkwell, and it'll really set the mood.

In Chapter 8, we will walk together into the ancient 2,100-year-old vortex site. This place needs far more attention. There are many old carvings still buried underground. This is an old place with lots of information. The old carvings are very strange. One symbol looks like a man, but it's not. It's actually speaking of the underground magnetic ley lines.

ANCIENT BOULDERS SOLSTICE SITE

This ancient solstice site was first found when Beth and I were out for one of our first mile or two hikes we took regularly when we first moved up here thirteen years ago. It's a beautiful walk through the old-growth oak trees. This trail led up a steep trail up and over to the back of the dam. It was a cool horseback trail from the parking lot. Go up to the outhouse park; there will be two trails in. Take the one on the right. The solstice boulder site is three hundred feet or so on the right. Take the book with you; you'll find it. There were ten or twenty huge boulders there. The slab standing up against the oak pointing to it is in the book. Be there on the summer equinox. The setting sun will come right down on top of it. You can almost see your parked car from the site. I did make a cool VHS of each phase of the year. I can burn a DVD. I explained everything. It came out nice. There's still tons of work on working out the matrix of this beautiful place. This site leads back to another site up the road you came in to park. Back up the windy road by the quarry entrance two or three miles up the road leads to a place called Bear Cove, easy to find. Go in and park.

Hike in five or six hundred feet or so till you cross a small creek. Look to your right. You'll see an old dried-up waterfall with huge boulders. Go over the falls on the trail to the right. Head in two or three hundred feet or so. You'll barely see a small house or cabin through the brush. Go left till you see the two-story-high ancient monolithic boulders standing up there—awesome. There is some kind of connection to the site at the quarry site point on the way back to Bear Cove. The energy at the Bear Cove monolithic site is off the charts. I love it back there. The site gives me goosebumps. I am trying to take this sight all in. I've got to get back there again. Okay, let's get back to the quarry site. What you can find out in the history of this place in Valley Springs archives is that long ago. It was named the Trail of Tears. The tribes fought over this place. It made sense to me that the ancient solstice site was a sacred site to the tribes. They found plenty of skulls there. May they rest in peace. Let me say this about the Bear Cove site. You're very secluded back there. I do not go in there to that area without hardware. It's Bear Country. The site is one of a kind. Be safe back there.

I have a kind of eye for locating ancient sites, so when we first saw them, they just didn't look right. They somehow looked out of place on the left side of the area. They built a high dirt level to hold back the water. It protected the Trail of Skulls area. The creek water was channeled down the creek when they opened the dam for overflow. But there was something else going on here; you just got that strange feeling there was more to this than met the eye. I brought back my compass and an angled iron. I wanted to square things up with a few measurements. The blocks in the center were almost perfectly square. They were lined up with the equinox winter and summer solstice. Also, there was a boulder in the center that was lined up with the compass—north, south, east, west with a half of a degree. I doubt very much that there was a dozer operator who would take the time to line things up. He would need a host of instruments to get that accomplished. In the summer equinox, there is a really cool huge slab of rock leaning against another smaller boulder. At the top of the standing slab of rock, there's a kind of buck horn site on top. During the equinox, the sundrops exactly between the sites are beautiful to witness, a real feeling of being balanced with the earth, something that you can't get from today's technology.

This site is really cool. If I'd be blessed to be able to find these sites, it would connect me back to the past, and then I can learn. This place is really much older than the old natives of the past; this was put together by the ancient ones. The hunter-gatherer natives wouldn't have wasted time with this site. They were too busy looking for food. Life was tough. And they wouldn't have had the equipment. These boulders are three tons and more. So now it's left to collect more time as it's done for maybe thousands of years serving a people long ago. Only they will know the true meaning of this sacred place. It's cool that they were connected to this place in the years to come. It had great meaning.

Is there hidden knowledge here right in front of our noses? The technology it took to move these huge boulders in place, did they use some kind of technology like a coral castle? I hope we can learn new technology maybe even given to us from the star family so we can't get ripped off. I do not want to be left in the Dark Ages. This is how it would take to get help for all were a hundred years behind schedule. Will we be a people who can do the right thing? I think so. I know all of us wish and pray for our seventh generation. This ancient site makes me think of Pueblo Bonito in Chaco Canyon, the way those ancient people built and laid out those buildings lined up. With the sun, stars, moon, and earth, they had a superior knowledge of astronomy and lined-up star systems.

There are folks who believe we came from Neanderthal man cave monkeys. This is a lie. If you look at the pyramids, Chaco Canyon, and Angkor Wat, you will understand that these were sophisticated people. You were not made from a caveman or a monkey. You are created in the image of the great spirit, God, the father of all life. You are much, much more than modern-day man would tell you. Life is much more sophisticated and complex. God doesn't make junk. Remember, we talked about the planet. It is like a beautiful Swiss watch, and that 7.83 Hz is the same in us as in our atmosphere. Does that really seem like something in common with monkeys or cavemen? Yeshua said, "You can do greater things than I, but you must have faith." He meant you, not monkeys or troglodytes, and let me say this. They talk about evolution. Think of your great-great-grandfathers, even people as far back as the ancient Sumerians. Ask yourself how much we have changed in the past. Six thousand years, really. Do we have three eyes, thirteen toes, twelve fingers, two brains? No.

Our outer bodies can only age from what we once was. However, our God-given gift is our spirit inward can be changed. Thank you, Yeshua. Do not let modern-day man talk you into the god of technology. You are far greater than any man-made gadget. These are just toys to keep us occupied. Draw close to the spirit, and the spirit will draw close to you. Believe me, I love cool high-tech just like the next guy. But I put God first and then all the other cool stuff next. Let's get balanced.

Well, I'm soon to walk us both into my Bigfoot encounters. I will testify again that every story I'm writing is absolutely true. This is not a book of fiction. I wouldn't waste my money or your time. Let's move on to my Bigfoot encounters. I think you'll like them. See you in Chapter 9.

CHAPTER 9

Bigfoot Encounters

I'm going to throw you a curveball in this chapter. I'm going to walk you through my Bigfoot encounters. And let me digress a little for a minute. I have played a major role in more things from world treasures to Planet X to uncovering ancient sites, also dealing with Bigfoot. There's a lot I can't go into, too much for different reasons, and I also need to keep my word to people. So please forgive me; it's best for all.

At the time of my Bigfoot encounter, I lived up in Arnold, California, after my two years working as a YACC (Young Adult Conservation Core), in the forest service. Those folks were the coolest, kindest people you could ever want to be around. There's a whole story in those days. My leaders were the greatest. God, I miss those folks. Then after six months of setting chokers for a logging outfit out of Sonora, California, I was feeling in for a good man with one arm who was working on the landing site cleaning up the logs with a chainsaw also branding the logs. He was off for a time with eye surgery. I never worked so hard in my life. Those one-inch-thick massive twenty-foot-long steel cables with their heavy bell end connection, I was dragging three of those up a heavily brushed hillside. There were some cool times like on those very cold mornings watching the CAT operator spray ether in that old D8 CAT pony motor to get that old pony motor to fire up. Once we got her fired up, that's when the work started.

Sorry for digressing a little. Let's get back to the boss of the woods. Okay, I had some time off, so I figured I'd pick up some supplies and head back to the deep woods for a night of peace and solitude. I picked up a nice T-bone steak, two six-packs of beer, and a pint of vodka. I figured I would get plastered and just pass out in the back of that old '62 Dodge short bed pickup. She had a police interceptor motor in it with a mild cam. She sounded pretty cool. And I just came home the next day—let say I was twenty-three years old and wouldn't give my life to Christ for another two years. So, my brothers and sisters, you'll just have to hold on. I also had a 30-30 Winchester with a full box of shells strapped around my waist. I also brought my friend's big black Labrador with me. And when he got provoked, he could be absolutely vicious. He'd scare the heck out of me when he got hot. I was one of his best friends. He was a good dog, lovable as any good dog could be. So without giving up the safety of my Bigfoot brothers, I was just maybe two or three miles from home. I lived in a trailer park in Arnold, California. That's a long time gone now. The post office is in its place now, so let's get back to preparing camp. I had camp pretty much in good shape for the night.

I needed to collect a few more nice-sized boulders for the fire ring. This camp was covered in a heavy canopy of old-growth trees. All covered in heavy brush. About fifteen feet away was a beautiful running winding creek. The camp was beyond a perfect place. It was a sacred place, and I was soon about to find out why. I was on one knee, placing the last stone in the fire safety ring. The creek wound up the steep mountain ravine in and out of the trees. About a quarter mile up the mountain came this huge roar. This roar was equivalent to three or four brahma bulls. I've heard the lion's roar in the San Francisco Zoo; this roar was at least three of those put together. It got my immediate attention. Time stood still for a bit. When I have these off-the-charts moments, I have a simple way of keeping myself cool. To keep from panicking, I throw a little humor into things. I said out loud, "I didn't hear that," with a very short smile. I also realized quick that this place was also someone else's favorite place. So I told that old Labrador in a not-so-funny way, "If I hear that one more time, we're packing up and hitting the trail out of our little hideaway and this trip is done." Let me say that this roar had at least three different pitches to it. At first, a loud roar growl then a high-pitched shriek then all of it mixed together.

It was a one-of-a-kind animal, and I knew exactly what I was dealing with. So it let off another one of those spine-chilling yells a second time. And that was it for us. I kept my cool. Panicking has never worked for me whether I was fighting a forest fire up in the mountains for the forest service or chaining up with the big rig, having to climb the grade out of Butte, Montana, with a load of latex for Helena Montana in the winter. You can't say you're in control of seventy-eight thousand pounds under you on ice or anything else. If you panic, then you're out of control, so we packed up camp quietly and quickly but still stayed cool. Everything went well, but we were about a half of a mile headed out when I became absolutely scared to death. I just couldn't imagine that huge creature walking out in front of us way back in the woods. It made me terrified; that 30-30 looked like my Daisy popgun as a child. That surely wasn't going to help. It would have made things much worse. But it never showed itself to me, thank God. I remember praying, *God, please do not let it show itself to us.* We made it back home safely about two months prior. I had bought my first pistol, a 25-caliber. It wasn't much more than a glorified 22-caliber. Anyway, I just wanted to fire it once for a quick test. I had one shell in it, and I was close to our camp. We were, at the most, a half-mile away from there. So I pulled over and got out to fire a test round, and when I was ready to fire it, I couldn't figure out what to shoot at. I know it sounds silly, but it's true. I think that time for me was a good lesson to be learned ahead. So I was up shooting that 25-caliber into a huge pine tree. After I shot, I felt really stupid for doing that to that to that beautiful living tree. I believe I was probably being watched at that time, so I always felt like I owed them for not scaring me half to death.

Years later, I wanted to take my wife up to that campsite. We were in her Toyota. It was too low to the ground; we were bottoming out with the deep ruts. She was getting a little upset, so I figured it would be good to turn around. I was feeling a little upset, remembering what happened there years before. This was about two years ago. We tried that, but I've learned a great respect for these people of the woods. I had two more encounters, at least one more. For sure, the second one, I was in the trailer at home. This was about five weeks after the first encounter. It was a late night, dark and cold. The Labrador was out on the porch. The lab went completely nuts. I mean he was hot. He never got like this. Arnold is a small town, and he knew everyone. He looked like a fearless black timber wolf.

That's what I mean about that friend of man; he would scare the heck out of me. So I called him in the trailer and ran and got out my single-shot 12-gauge Savage. I sled the barrow out of my sliding glass door and set one off. I was scared, young, and stupid. I knew that whatever got him so hot wasn't good at all. I believe Bigfoot is very intelligent, and they also can find out where you live. Never bring a weapon of any kind on a Bigfoot camping. They never travel alone, and there's a good chance you'll never make it home. But all I know the boss of the woods just was trying to come around to pay a visit. I have grown up a whole lot since those days. I will share with you my third encounter. I will not tell the area where this is. I can't risk endangering this tribe of forest people. There is a place on the west coast where there is a family of Bigfoot. We took the family in for an overnight sleepover. It's a beautiful hike.

There are also two places where Drake left these things. We were in this area now, and then these forest people brought me a freshly killed rabbit. They have the ability to read your minds and judge your character, what kind of person you are. They also get help from ET. This is why Native Americans say when Bigfoot travels at night, he's always seen with a lantern following him. The meaning of orb lights come to mind.

So think twice about pulling the trigger next time. So anyway the last time we hiked, we were all in a single-file line hiking in to camp. These Bigfoot are so fast and quiet. The way they can move is almost unworldly. The trail was only two feet wide. Beth was ahead of me about seventy feet. The rest of the group was way up the trail. I was last. The hills were kicking my butt. I was so out of shape from running the line with my big rig. There were lots of setting driving trucks. The trail had five-foot-tall stalks. If you laid something in front of you on the trail, there was no way the next person on the trail would miss it. They would have to step over it. When I reached the spot where she just was, there in front at my feet was a freshly killed cottontail rabbit lying across the trail. I knew this was a gift from the forest people, so I left the rabbit behind. There was no firewood at this camp at all. Also, I didn't want to gross out the ladies. We bought sandwiches for breakfast, lunch, and dinner. But I sure did get the message. I kept quiet about all the signs in and out of the trip. There were also tree snaps, a territorial thing, and one time, one was right behind a huge boulder. This one was letting me know they meant no harm to us whatsoever. Next time, I'll bring enough sandwiches for all of us.

I'm a little uncomfortable even writing this part. I want them kept safe. They are forest people; they want to be left alone, occasionally making friends and trading things. They are like us; there's good and bad. This group knew we were the deer people, and we were where the deer were; there was a kind of balance here.

So back to the trail. When I got a chance to talk to Beth alone, I asked her, "Honey, did you see that fresh rabbit kill down on the bottom trail?"

She said, "No."

There is no way she could have not seen that; she would have had to step over it. It was in less than two minutes that I found it. I'm told that Bigfoot is a creation of my ancestors of Atlantis, half-bear, half-human. I have been told many things about Atlantis of the past, some good and sometimes a full-blown nightmare. I have a few good close brothers that I can open up to about these kinds of things. I definitely don't bring these topics up at church. My ancestors had high technology, but we began to get too much into DNA and began splicing DNA together with humans and animals. This started all their troubles. I got terribly out of hand. They made lots of enemies, I'm told by spirit. This might be a little hard for the New Age people.

At one time, we had a sweet visitor. She was a beautiful princess who came from another star system. She was on a peace mission on behalf of both our time lines. We took her and surgically removed her head and attached it on a four-legged animal of some kind; that's all I'm told. When I shared this with a close brother in a small café in San Rafael, California, I broke down and cried. He responded by saying, "Darn it, Darrell. Now you made me cry." A brother like that you can talk with your soul; he's one of a kind.

So this is why I talked back in my UFO encounters. Are we really ready to handle high technology? Can we really handle it with responsibility thinking about the future of the seventh generations to come? Maybe it's better we keep our feet on the ground only God knows we should pray about it. We can change this planet and balance her again. This is why it's so important to do what Yeshua said on the sermon on the mount. Your prayers are sacred when your spirit connects with the great spirit. This day and age is leading us away from any connection with Jesus, leading us away with technology and dreams of lots of money. If you have the Yeshua spirit in your heart, you are already rich and powerful. Our people, young and old, are being led away from the spirit connection with our Creator. Don't be misled away from who you really are, a God-created child of this Mother Earth. Amen.

We will never get the technology that we need to have real growth for the people as long as we put technology first and God and the earth second—this is like putting the cart before the horse. It will never balance with nature and the awesome, beautiful Mother Earth; she's a spaceship traveling around our sun. Our treasure is right in front of our face, and some of us can't see it. It's time to understand the Native Americans and their ways of caring for the earth and animals and of course the people of the earth. Do you have the strength and ability not to be judgmental, or are you so brainwashed with tunnel vision that you can't learn anymore? Are you a know-it-all? I'm sure you're not. The world is full of fantastic, beautiful people trying to put all the pieces of this life together like myself. The more I see and witness and learn, the more I realize I don't know anything. This world is a magnificent place to be filled with wondrous things. These things will never make life dull. Let's get our ducks back in order and trust Christ. His spirit will never leave you, never forsake you. Stay grounded and you will learn. This life will never stop providing for all of us, but you must make wish decisions. This world is not a playground. We're going to have to buckle down and take the bull by the horns. Thank you, Mom.

CHAPTER 10

Why I'm Writing This Book

When I was a very young Christian, I was heavily instructed by the spirit. I was reminded that Jesus looked in the soul, not the face. I had to train myself in my own way to talk to a person's soul, not their face. After I became more spiritual, this technique got stronger as time went on. After I was becoming more like Yeshua, this technique got stronger and stronger. In no time, I could treat everyone with the love of Christ. I didn't care if you had lots of money or no money or had to walk with or without crutches. I could be myself again. Everyone was so different. This helped me to get closer to my Creator. I always had this gift, but it needed a lot of fine-tuning. A lot of my friends in grammar school had deformed hands or had to walk with crutches. This didn't bother me one bit. In fact, I thought they were very cool and just plain nice. I could see their soul as young as the third grade. So most of this was natural, but I was to find out in the near future that was not natural at all in or out of church. I had many reality checks in the land of plenty. I became a little bitter in church. These folks… I didn't fit in with the rich. I guess I was thinking everyone was like Jesus. Boy, was I mistaken. Well, after years of following the great spirit, he has helped me understand and to love all. Young people, guard your heart in and out of church.

I don't care what land you're from; you and I are family. I've been writing this book every day for about eight weeks or so. Maybe I'll start slowly to wind down on the book. I will see how your response turns out to the book. I will see if you're ready for this kind of talk. Maybe this will be the one and only book from me. I'd like to see a nice movie made up about Planet Nibiru. After all, I am an eyewitness. I would like people to experience what I went through. I had a strong feeling to share these absolutely true accounts of my life. I have to leave out the best stories at this time of my life. This is a complex and complicated world we live in. When I read the Bible, I stick mostly to the red letters with exception of the Psalms. When I jump around, I start to pick up judgmental spirits. I'm an empath, and my psychic abilities are off the charts. This is why I'm not too keen on today's churches or discussing someone's views on what I should be doing. I know what to do. Just keep listening to God, Yeshua, and the spirits that can give life to the dead. We're trying to put some pictures for you guys. We'll see how difficult it's going to be. This is my first book. I have no idea about writing a book, so I will be praying on what to do. Thank you before I forget to say it. The proceeds will go toward Deer Feed. Bless you from the deer people.

Please do not think I'm steering you away from church. I'm trying to bring you closer to the Creator. We are changing rapidly today. The Pentagon is coming out of the closet about UFOs, that they are real. Technology is out there on the rise. I'm concerned for all ages of people. I've always mustered up the guts to tell family or neighbors or people I've meet at the job sites. I would feel like a coward not to share the truth of my encounters. So the heck with those folks who laugh. I'm not here to win an award. But I have to say there's been a huge group of folks that I've been blessed to meet. There's hope that I keep going on and on about buried topics. I do love to go to church now and then, especially when I pick up the spirit; there's a lot of love going on there. And for those who stare with that cold glare of ungodliness, I just pray for them and then avoid them like at the plague. That kind of darkness can stick to you. Darkness can cause all kinds of pain. Someone should tell them it's rude to stare. You can unleash all kinds of hell with that look. So for forty-one years of loving God, I've dealt with all of it. Guard your heart.

So you can see I'm trying to keep the faith. The spirit of God is more than enough for me. People who have these kind of encounters are not cursed by the devil. You have been chosen to make a stand for God. He knew you would be strong enough, and he will stand with you through any encounter. Stay strong, my brothers and sisters. The stronger your faith, the more encounters you'll have of any kind. I'd like to share about these wild, off-the-scales encounters. I do not know for sure what these star brothers in there with off-the-charts high-tech crafts are really up to. All I can say is that I had to listen to my heart, and it's always left me feeling like I had such an overwhelming sense of peace. That's all I ever had to go with. I've always trusted my gut feeling; it's like a third eye. It's never let me down. This is my faith. I do not think Yeshua walked the earth. I *know* he walked the earth. The spirit in me is more powerful than any battle star ship. Keep God in your heart. Remember, he created the star crafts, so he allowed them to come into existence. I do not know if I'll ever see another star craft. If I do not, it's all good. Everything that happens in your life is prearranged. Nothing is a coincidence, so just do the back float. None of us will ever be able to figure out all of it. This will keep all of us learning that this is the Creator.

Nothing is created without his permission, nothing. So we're here and there, and all the other things that God put in this multiple universe is here. I need his spirit, guidance, and protection. This is how I face these encounters. I couldn't face these things without him. I do not see how people make it without God. I hope my book helps you. This is for you guys.

I'll get a little personal about my life for a bit. I met my wife in church. We both were Christians. It was instantly a huge hit, a bigtime crush. We were both head over heels in love, and if she knew I was writing this, she'd kick my butt. Anyway, I didn't want to rush things, so I waited till the second date before I asked her to marry me. After we dated a couple of months, we knew it would take place. But she said, "We'll date for one year without relations, and then and only then would there be a marriage." We both loved God. God was our stronghold, and we did wait. I'm glad we did. I didn't want to lose her. I wanted to spend the rest of my life with her. It's a good idea to wait before relations. Marriage is sacred; it's for life. All right, so it's been thirty-four years and we're still together. So put the spirit first, and you'll never go wrong.

I'm not going to share too much in this book about my true face-to-face encounter with an ancient black dragon. This took place in Kanab Utah at a place called Three Lakes. I was no more than three and a half feet from him. I was in a small two-man foot-paddle boat. It was guarding an ancient Aztec treasure. It showed itself to me. I didn't say a thing to anyone. It was very personal. I found out more about it when I watched the History Channel quest for dragons about a year later after that trip. It showed ancient pottery with this dragon on it saying it guards treasure. I know what I saw that day. This brother is related to the dragon on an Aztec temple pyramid in Mexico. Those are not feathers around its head; those are more like spikes. The one I met had at least thirty spikes around its head about two inches wide and two feet long. He had bright yellow eyes with piercing black pupils. The eyes were the size of silver dollars. From side to side, the head was about three or three and a half feet from spike to spike. If you weren't prepared to see this, you would easily go out of your mind.

I can pass any lie detector test. I told you that you were going to get double barrels in this book. I'm holding back. I don't know what you can handle. This book is not fiction. Well, it got kind of fun there for a minute. There was a huge thunderstorm going on here. The thunder beings were pushing me to give it to ya.

Mom passed away over a year ago. She was probably riding one of the lightning bolts. Man, that woman was always behind me. I really miss her. It's not good when they're gone. You do not know what you've got till it's gone. Always love you, Mom. We will meet again. Her favorite time in life, she said, is when I would pick her up and take her to the ranch we had in Copperopolis, California. She loved to dig ditches and help me build the place up. She took many pictures of me showing off on my old TD 61 bulldozer. This bulldozer once belonged to the Peterson family of Peterson Caterpillar and was painted up to look like a D2Cat, but it was international. Funny how things wind up. Mom, this chapter is dedicated to you. I'm fighting the tears back.

I just want to stop and thank all of you wonderful people with good hearts. Without you, this world wouldn't be the same. Keep on being you.

Okay, let's move on to the last chapter of the book. I'm starting to miss you already. Let's slide into Chapter 11. I hope I got enough down in there. Like I say, I'm not a writer. I'm just a man who loves God and good, kind people.

CHAPTER 11

Tribute to My Trucker Family

I would like to take some time out to thank my trucker family, my absolutely brave men and women of our trucking industry. Thank you for all your hard work in helping make this a better world. Thank you for chaining up and risking your lives hauling loads over those snow-capped summits. Thank you for tarping those expensive machinery loads. Thank you, all you tomato haulers. I never complained with the tomato juice on my front windshield. You are close to my heart. Grampa and Uncle Joe farmed six hundred acres way back in the day. Thank you to all of you who hauled those very expensive permit loads. Thank you to all of you hauling food grade with those long sixteen- to one-hundred-hour resets. You are amazing. Thank you to all you lowbed heavy equipment haulers for loading those huge caterpillars on a slippery wet winter deck. That's the coolest-looking load this one has ever seen. Thank you to you folks that are hauling those houses on wheels. The messages you sent me went off the charts. Those loads were foundation loads for the dreams to come. Thank you for loading and unloading all those Hazmat loads. My heart and safety will be with you always. And thank you to you reefer drivers hauling all those beautiful loads of food. We would not make it as a whole without you.

God bless any truck driver. I hung with you for thirty-nine and a half years. I had to surrender—my health is not the greatest—but I do not go a day without thinking about my family on the open roads.

I still have my CB going in my little four-wheeler flatbed. My handle is little brother. So I'll just say, at the coming and going of the White Buffalo Cafe, we will have peace. Just as now we are going through hard times, we must join together in peace. The White Buffalo Cafe was born on August 20, 1994. My white Peterbilt was custom-built for me in 1994.

Nothing in life is a coincidence. Trust in the Creator. United we stand; divided we fall. We will overcome, my brothers and sisters. This dark force of greed will pass, and we will take back this beautiful land for the truth and majesty that she is like this natural planet perfectly put in motion around the sun, rotating in perfect harmony through the galaxy like a beautiful Swiss watch, set in perfect timing by the great spirit to fulfill his will. This is the way of our gift from him, not control and greediness. The way of greed will never go forward. It will be rejected and tossed out when you see the Native Americans' land being put back, their God-given right, and their families put in the healing time. Then you'll know we're on the right track again. We must help give back to these sacred caretakers of the land to put back our learning process, all of us together. This is the healing secret given to you now.

We must show the great spirit we have the compassion for our earth and the people on her to care for this gift of God's earth and all the animals on it. We must care for the people of Africa's land, and then the people will be healed. We must care for the Native Americans, and the United States will be healed. See how easy it is? Even a child could figure this out. We all must join our forces around the world. Blessed are the peacemakers for they shall inherit the earth. This is what the billionaires of the earth should invest in, then their plans would be positive, not negative, and they would go forward. With all their money, they can't figure that out. Let's get back to common sense here. You're a powerful person. What you think about, how you treat each other, you have the ability to change time lines. Let's stay focused on being positive, responsible people, not tailgating, troubled people. Use your head. If you want nice things to happen, then do nice things. It's up to you. You can change things.

I had a close friend, a highly decorated Green Beret. He did four deployments in Vietnam. He had more sharp metal wounds, bullet wounds. And the word was when he was on a riverboat as a gunner on the 50 cal., they were hit by a rocket. It blew him out of the gunner's seat and up near the shore, face down in the river Tuli's. This injury removed part of his skull. He made me look at all the injuries. He knew I was an empath. An empath has the ability to understand and share the feelings of another. Finally, I'd have to say, "Bob, please no more."

One time, we were at the old bar Whiskey River in Arnold, California. I was sitting to his right. I looked over at him. His eyes were black. He would get in that combat mood. I called it the thing that made him a fierce warrior. He scared the heck out of me, but then just like that, he would look over at me with those big blue eyes and a wonderful smile. He'd say, "You know, Darrell, it don't cost you one iota to be nice." I might say they did a beautiful job on repairing his injuries. Now you can see why we were friends. Everyone loved him. Most people called him Big Hat. I was at his place many times. I'd seen him when he was young in his pictures, and his uniform had a ton of medals. This was back in the day when I lived in Arnold, California, around the time of my Bigfoot encounters.

I feel like it's time again to stop and thank all the good, kind, loving people of the world. You know who you are. I want to say "Thank you, God," for the souls who walk truly as peacemakers. You truly are blessed, and this chapter is dedicated to all of you. Whatever your relationship with God, you are loved and respected. Thank you for being you. God bless all of us. May we all get closer to understanding God.

I'm having an empty feeling that I'm leaving you. I've never written a book before. I want to give my heart to this book, but I never knew what putting my heart on paper would feel like. I understand why the Navajo women would weave a spirit line in their rugs when they were finished. This is so their spirits wouldn't get trapped in it. This gives putting your heart into something a whole new meaning.

I just want to say this book is dedicated to all my brothers and sisters all around the world who have had encounters and sightings, the ones who love God and are being judged as if the dark side is somehow in league with you. This is horse crap. You were chosen because God knew you could deal with these issues. All of us have gifts, and sometimes, they're not the same. So hang in there; we all must deal with what we were dealt. Let's practice the sermon on the mount together. We will have creators help the world of wealth-controlling powers that would like to make you into an under-control robot, dragging you far away from the spiritual connection that keeps you grounded. This way, you are more easily led away. You'll believe whatever they say as truth. This is why you must listen to your heart; be your own leader. You are a powerful being. This is what you are here for: to learn to be you. Don't let technology steer you away. Let's get our ducks in order.

It's January 14, 2023, and it's been nice writing the book. We're getting a huge storm, lots of wind and rain. Thank God the wind blew the XT 500 over twice. We need to keep praying for God's will with the rain filling our reservoir and dams. When we join in prayer for the issues of this planet, things will change. This is why they want to spread division in the people. Stay strong in doing the right thing. There are millions of people like us who feel the same way. We want to restore our beautiful planet to the way it was and even better than it was with good-paying jobs, fair food and gas prices, equality for all, and most of all, a good, strong, trustworthy government that the people can be proud of. This should be and will be in the days to come. No more buffalo chip lies.

So I'm glad I'm trusting Yeshua and trusting the Holy Spirit of the Creator. This was put in my life first. It was my way to be faithful, trustworthy, and true to God and my wife. Marriage is a sacred thing. So all these different encounters that took place just give me more to be grateful for. I will keep praying, knowing that God is bigger than my encounters. He is the author of my encounters and my life. I feel privileged to bring this small part of my life. God bless all of you. May the peace of Christ be upon you all. Blessings, Darrell.

ABOUT THE AUTHOR

    Darrell is a retired truck driver. He drove for thirty-nine and a half years. Everything in this book are true things that he has been through. He has been a Christian for forty-one years and has seen a lot and has not lost his faith. He has written this book to help people keep their hope and faith in God whatever happens.